Wildflower SAMPLER

Lynda Milligan
& Nancy Smith

Book Production

Sharon Holmes – Editor, Technical Illustrator
Susan Johnson – Quilt & Project Designer, Photo Stylist
Lexie Foster – Graphic & Quilt Designer, Photography
Christine Scott – Editorial Assistant
Sandi Fruehling – Copy Reader
Brad Bartholomew – Photographer

Thanks

Sewers – Jane Dumler, Ann Petersen, Katie Wells, Christine Scott
Quilters – Ann Petersen, Jane Dumler
Longarm Quilters – Merrie Martin Jones, Debra Geissler, Kay Morrison
Crate & Barrel – Photography in their beautiful store at
8505 Park Meadows Center Drive, Lone Tree, Colorado 80124

Every effort has been made to ensure that the information in this book is accurate. Due to individual skills, conditions, and tools, we cannot be responsible for any losses, injuries, or other damages that may result from its use.

POSSIBILITIES®

Fabric Designers for Avlyn, Inc. • Publishers of Possibilities® Books
Home of Great American Quilt Factory Inc.
www.greatamericanquilt.com • www.possibilitiesquilt.com
1.800.474.2665

Wildflower Sampler
©2007 Lynda Milligan & Nancy Smith

ISBN 1-880972-61-1

Wildflower Sampler

76 x 90"   12" Blocks   Please read through all directions before beginning.

The quilt in the photo was made for a Block of the Month program with different fabrics in each monthly kit. Consequently we used over 90 fabrics to make the quilt. For this book, we have combined some of the fabrics to reduce the number to less than 40, which also decreases the total yardage needed. See chart in box below. ***In this box, specific fabrics are listed for the applique, but fabrics can be used as desired in blocks.*** Therefore, it is advisable to cut all applique pieces before beginning to cut for the blocks. The chart includes plenty of fabric to make the quilt, even if the minimum number of fabrics listed for each color is purchased. If desired, add a few eighth-yard cuts, fat eighths, or scraps to increase the total number of fabrics. The eight fabrics for the center panel, sashing, and borders can be used for blocks also, but cut the pieces for these major parts first, then use the scraps in blocks.

Yardage Choose fabric with 42" usable width.

Center panel background	¼ yd each of 5 light blues	Fusible web	5 yd
Center panel border	⅜ yd medium purple	Binding	¾ yd
Sashing	1¼ yd medium blue	Backing	5¾ yd
Outer border	2⅜ yd dark blue	Batting	82 x 96"
Applique & blocks	see chart below		

Fabrics for Applique & Blocks

Color	# of Fabrics	Yards	Use
Dark blue	1	⅓ yd	blocks
Medium dark blue	1	½ yd	columbines, bellflowers; blocks
Medium blue	1	½ yd	columbines, bellflowers; blocks
	1	¼ yd	blocks
Light blue	2-3	⅓ yd each	1 for columbines; blocks
Turquoise	2-3	¼ yd each	1 for star flowers; blocks
Dark red-purple	1	⅜ yd	asters; blocks
	2-3	¼ yd each	blocks
Medium red-purple	1-2	¼ yd each	blocks
Medium purple	2-3	¼ yd each	blocks
Light purple	2	¼ yd each	blocks
Dark pink	1-2	¼ yd each	blocks
Light pink	1	¼ yd	blocks
Choose yellow-greens rather than blue-greens			
Dark green	1	½ yd	stems, vine, leaves A & B
Medium green	1	⅓ yd	stems, leaves C & D; blocks
	1-2	¼ yd each	blocks
Medium light green	1	½ yd	stems, leaves E & F; blocks
Light green	2	¼ yd each	leaves A & B veins; blocks
Orange	2	¼ yd each	star flower centers, berries; blocks
Medium gold	1-2	¼ yd each	1 for bow; blocks
Light gold	1	¼ yd	bow
Medium yellow	1	⅜ yd	flower centers
White	1	⅜ yd	columbines; meadow roses

Continued on page 4

3

Wildflower Sampler

Continued from page 2

Cutting
Cut strips selvage to selvage unless otherwise noted.

Center panel background — 3 pieces 5x36½" center pieces
2 pieces 4¾x36½" outside pieces

Center panel border — 2 pieces 2½x36½" sides
2 pieces 2½x26½" top/bottom

Sashing — 14 strips 2½" wide

Outer border — 4 strips 9½" wide
cut on lengthwise grain

Blocks & applique — see pages 5-11, 44-48
5 columbines
10 & 8 reversed side-view columbines
10 asters
8 large star flowers
3 small star flowers
11 meadow roses
10 bellflowers
4 & 4 reversed leaf A
3 leaf B
1 & 1 reversed leaf C
8 & 8 reversed leaf D
3 & 2 reversed leaf E
16 & 16 reversed leaf F
12 berries
1 bow

Binding — 9 strips 2½" wide

Directions
Use ¼" seam allowance unless otherwise noted.

1. CENTER PANEL: Stitch center pieces together, 3 wider ones in center, others at each side. Press. Stitch side border pieces to panel. Press. Stitch top and bottom border pieces to panel. Press. Panel measures 26½x40½" including seam allowances.

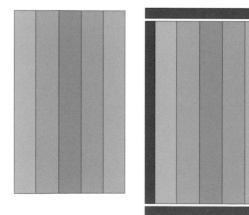

Applique bouquet to center panel, centered in each direction. See pages 44-46 for patterns, page 47 for layout diagrams and directions.

2. BLOCKS: See pages 5-11.

3. SASHING: Cut the following and use the pieces as noted on the diagram.
   a. Crosscut 4 strips into 10 pieces 12½" long.
   b. Trim 2 strips to 40½" long.
   c. Stitch 3 strips end to end. Press. Cut 2 pieces 54½" long.
   d. Stitch 2 strips end to end. Press. Repeat. Cut 1 piece 68½" long from each.
   e. Stitch 3 strips end to end. Press. Cut 2 pieces 58½" long.

4. OUTSIDE BORDER: Cut side borders to fit quilt. Stitch to quilt. Press. Repeat at top and bottom. Applique border. See pages 44-46 for patterns, page 48 for layout diagrams and directions.

5. LAYER & QUILT: Piece backing vertically to same size as batting. Layer and quilt as desired. Trim backing and batting even with top.

6. BIND: Stitch binding strips end to end. Press in half lengthwise, wrong sides together. Bind quilt using ⅜" seam allowance.

4

Wildflower Sampler
Block 1

12″ block

Colors in cutting chart below are suggestions. Use fabrics as desired. Paper piecing pattern on page 43.

Cutting *Cut in half diagonally.

Dark pink	paper pieced	side units
Light blue	paper pieced	side units
	*2 squares 4⅞″	corner units
Medium green	*2 squares 4⅞″	corner units
Orange	4 squares 2½″	center unit
Med blue	1 square 4½″	center unit

Directions Use ¼″ seam allowance.

1. Make 1 block following diagrams. Press.

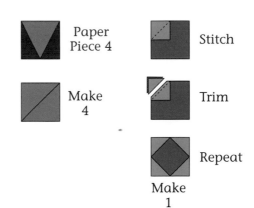

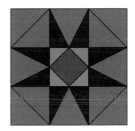

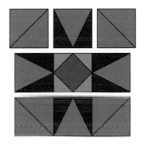

Wildflower Sampler
Block 2

12″ block

Colors in cutting chart below are suggestions. Use fabrics as desired.

Cutting *Cut in half diagonally.

Medium red-purple	*2 squares 3⅞″	side
Light purple	*2 squares 3⅞″	background
	8 squares 3½″	background
Light pink	*2 squares 3⅞″	center
Dark blue	*2 squares 3⅞″	center

Directions Use ¼″ seam allowance.

1. Make 1 block following diagrams. Press.

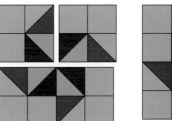

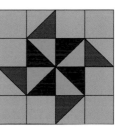

Wildflower Sampler
Block 3

12″ block

Colors in cutting chart below are suggestions. Use fabrics as desired.

Cutting *Cut in half diagonally.

Medium green	*8 squares 2⅞″	outer background
	4 squares 2½″	outer background
Dark red-purple	*8 squares 2⅞″	outer points
Light green	*4 squares 2⅞″	inner background
	4 squares 2½″	inner background
Med red-purple	*4 squares 2⅞″	inner points
Turquoise	1 square 4½″	center

Directions Use ¼″ seam allowance.

1. Make 1 block following diagrams. Press.

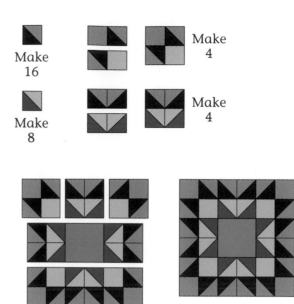

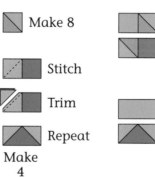

Wildflower Sampler
Block 4

12″ block

Colors in cutting chart below are suggestions. Use fabrics as desired.

Cutting *Cut in half diagonally.

Light blue	*4 squares 2⅞″	background
	4 squares 2½″	background
	4 pieces 2½ x 4½″	background
Medium gold	*4 squares 2⅞″	corner unit
Orange	4 squares 2½″	corner unit
Light green	8 squares 2½″	side unit
Turquoise	4 pieces 2½ x 4½″	side unit
Med dark blue	1 square 4½″	center

Directions Use ¼″ seam allowance.

1. Make 1 block following diagrams. Press.

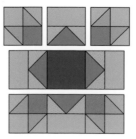

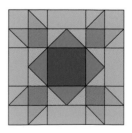

Wildflower Sampler
Block 5

12″ block

Colors in cutting chart below are suggestions. Use fabrics as desired.

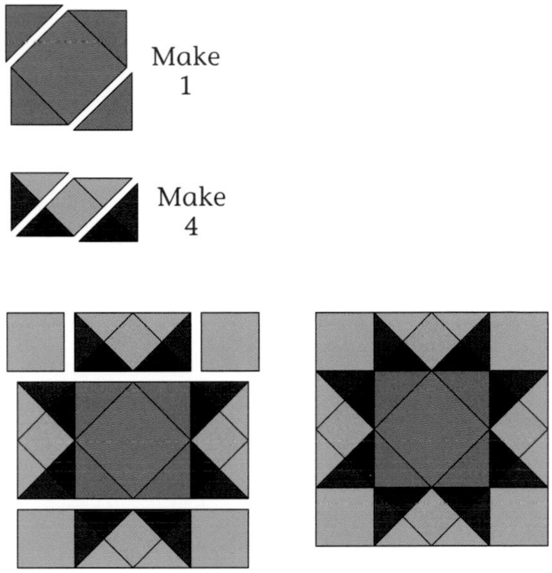

Cutting *Cut in half diagonally. **Cut in quarters diagonally.

Medium green	1 square 4¾″	center unit
Medium blue	*2 squares 3⅞″	center unit
Dark blue	**2 squares 4¼″	side unit
Dark red-purple	**2 squares 4¼″	side unit
Light blue	4 squares 2⅝″	side unit
Turquoise	**2 squares 4¼″	side unit
	4 squares 3½″	corners

Directions Use ¼″ seam allowance.

1. Make 1 block following diagrams. Press.

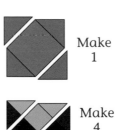
Make 1

Make 4

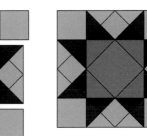

Wildflower Sampler
Block 6

12″ block

Colors in cutting chart below are suggestions. Use fabrics as desired.

Cutting *Cut in half diagonally. **Cut in quarters diagonally.

Dark blue	1 square 3½″	center unit
Light blue	*2 squares 3″	center unit
Dark red-purple	*4 squares 3″	corner unit
Light purple	4 squares 3½″	corner unit
	**1 square 7¼″	side triangles
Medium blue	*2 squares 3⅞″	corner unit
Medium gold	*4 squares 3″	corner unit

Directions Use ¼″ seam allowance.

1. Make 1 block following diagrams. Press.

Make 1

Make 4

Make 4

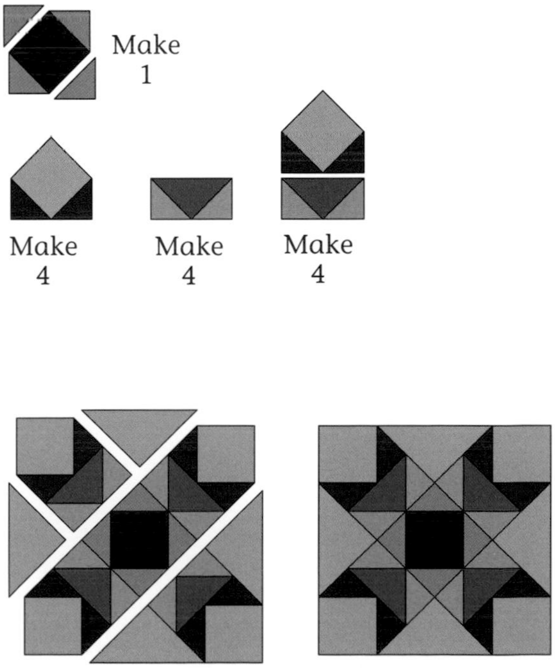

Make 4

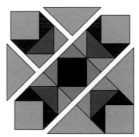

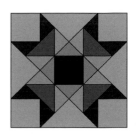

Wildflower Sampler
Block 7

12″ block

Colors in cutting chart below are suggestions. Use fabrics as desired.

Cutting *Cut in half diagonally. **Cut in quarters diagonally.

Medium purple	*2 squares 4⅞″	center unit
Orange	**1 square 5¼″	center unit
Turquoise	**1 square 5¼″	center unit
Med light green	*8 squares 2⅞″	side units
Dark pink	*8 squares 2⅞″	side units
	4 squares 2½″	corners

Directions Use ¼″ seam allowance.

1. Make 1 block following diagrams. Press.

Make 4

Make 1

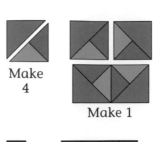

Make 16   Make 4

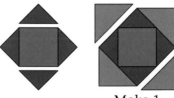

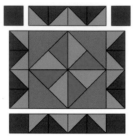

Wildflower Sampler
Block 8

12″ block

Colors in cutting chart below are suggestions. Use fabrics as desired.

Cutting *Cut in half diagonally.

Turquoise	1 square 4½″	center unit
Med red-purple	*2 squares 3¾″	center unit
Light purple	*2 squares 4⅞″	center unit
Med light green	*6 squares 2⅞″	sides, corners
	4 pieces 2½ x 4½″	sides
Dark red-purple	*6 squares 2⅞″	sides, corners

Directions Use ¼″ seam allowance.

1. Make 1 block following diagrams. Press.

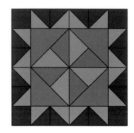

Make 1

Make 12   Make 4

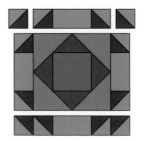

Wildflower Sampler
Block 9

12″ block

Colors in cutting chart below are suggestions. Use fabrics as desired. Paper piecing pattern on page 43.

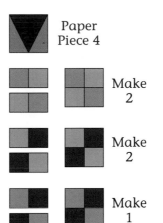

Paper Piece 4

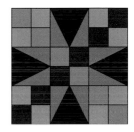

Make 2

Make 2

Make 1

Cutting

Dark blue	paper pieced	side units
Light blue	paper pieced	side units
Light pink	8 squares 2½″	corner units
Med light green	6 squares 2½″	corners, center
Dark red-purple	6 squares 2½″	corners, center

Directions Use ¼″ seam allowance.

1. Make 1 block following diagrams. Press.

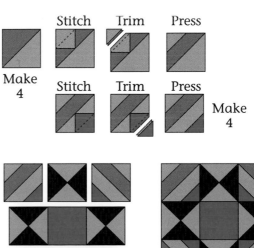

Wildflower Sampler
Block 10

12″ block

Colors in cutting chart below are suggestions. Use fabrics as desired.

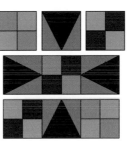

Make 4

Stitch   Trim   Press

Make 4

Stitch   Trim   Press

Make 4

Cutting *Cut in half diagonally. **Cut in quarters diagonally.

Dark red-purple	**2 squares 5¼″	side units
Medium gold	**1 square 5¼″	side units
Light blue	**1 square 5¼″	side units
	*2 squares 4⅞″	corner units
Light green	4 squares 2½″	corner units
Light purple	*2 squares 4⅞″	corner units
Turquoise	4 squares 2½″	corner units
	1 square 4½″	center

Directions Use ¼″ seam allowance.

1. Make 1 block following diagrams. Press.

Wildflower Sampler
Block 11

12″ block

Colors in cutting chart below are suggestions. Use fabrics as desired.

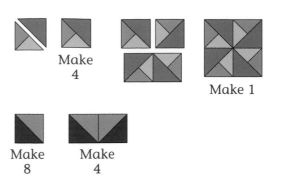

Make 4

Make 1

Cutting *Cut in half diagonally. **Cut in quarters diagonally.

Medium purple	*2 squares 3⅞″	center unit
Orange	**1 square 4¼″	center unit
Light green	**1 square 4¼″	center unit
Medium green	*4 squares 3⅞″	side units
	4 squares 3½″	corners
Dark blue	*4 squares 3⅞″	side units

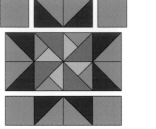

Make 8

Make 4

Directions Use ¼″ seam allowance.

1. Make 1 block following diagrams. Press.

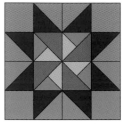

Wildflower Sampler
Block 12

12″ block

Colors in cutting chart below are suggestions. Use fabrics as desired.

Make 1

Cutting *Cut in half diagonally. **Cut in quarters diagonally.

Dark blue	1 square 4¾″	center unit
Medium gold	*2 squares 3⅞″	center unit
Light blue	*4 squares 3⅞″	side units
	4 squares 3½″	corners
Dark red-purple	**2 squares 4¼″	side units
Medium blue	**2 squares 4¼″	side units

Make 8

Make 4

Directions Use ¼″ seam allowance.

1. Make 1 block following diagrams. Press.

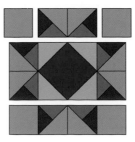

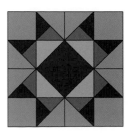

Wildflower Sampler
Block 13

12″ block

Colors in cutting chart below are suggestions. Use fabrics as desired.

Cutting
*Cut in half diagonally. **Cut in quarters diagonally.

Dark blue	*1 square 3⅞″	center unit
	**1 square 4¼″	side units
Light green	*2 squares 3⅞″	center unit
	**2 squares 4¼″	side units
	4 squares 3½″	corners
Orange	*1 square 3⅞″	center unit
Turquoise	**2 squares 4¼″	side units
Medium purple	**3 squares 4¼″	side units

Directions
Use ¼″ seam allowance.

1. Make 1 block following diagrams. Press.

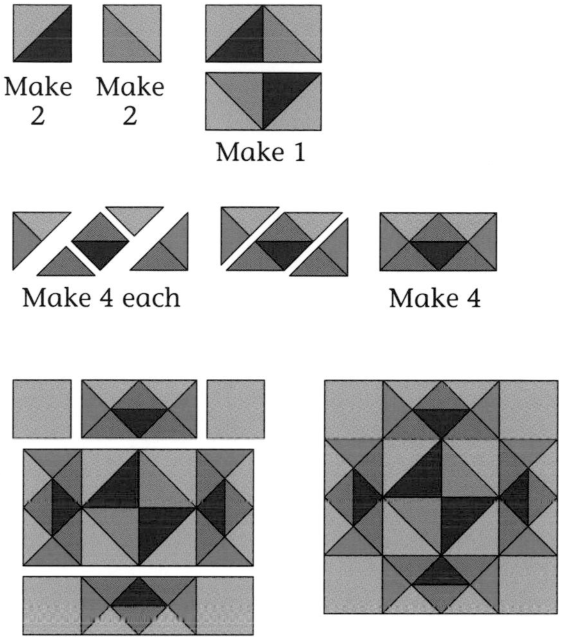

Make 2   Make 2

Make 1

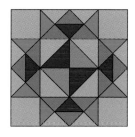

Make 4 each   Make 4

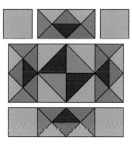

Wildflower Sampler
Block 14

12″ block

Colors in cutting chart below are suggestions. Use fabrics as desired.

Cutting
*Cut in half diagonally.

Light blue	*2 squares 3⅞″	background
	8 squares 3½″	background
Light green	*2 squares 3⅞″	star points
Orange	2 pieces 3½x6½″	star points
Med purple	2 pieces 3½x6½″	star points

Directions
Use ¼″ seam allowance.

1. Make 1 block following diagrams. Press.

Make 4   Stitch / Trim / Press   Make 2 / Make 2

Make 2   Make 2

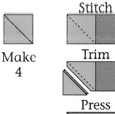

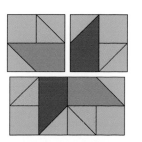
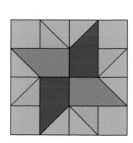

11

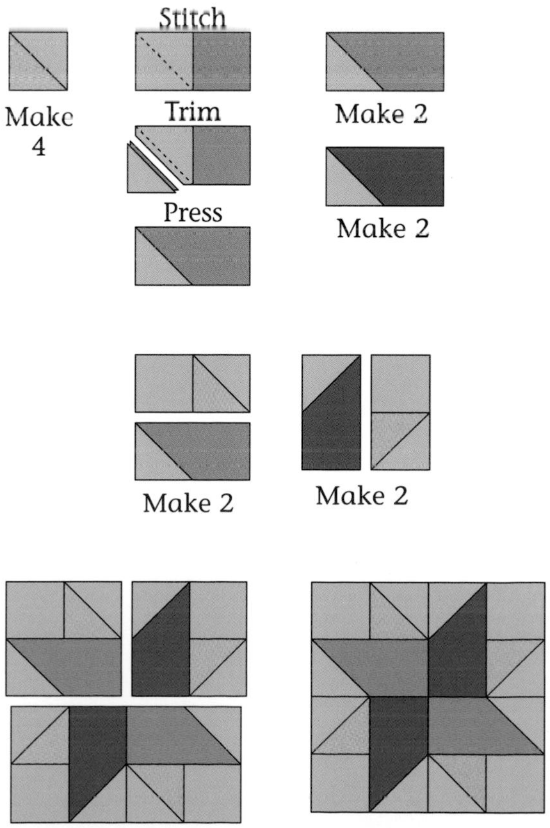

20 x 28″
For 1 standard size pillow

Make 28   Make 14

Yardage Choose fabrics with 42″ usable width.

Medium blue	¾ yd - main fabric
Light blue	¼ yd - applique background
Dark blue	⅙ yd - borders near applique
Light purple	¼ yd - triangle & edge borders
Yellow	⅛ yd - triangle border
Applique	⅛ yd each of 3 greens, 3 blues for columbines, 2 blues for bellflowers, 1 turquoise, 1 yellow, 1 white
Binding	⅛ yd
Backing	1⅜ yd
Batting	36 x 45″

Cutting Cut strips selvage to selvage.
*Cut in half diagonally.

Medium blue	1 piece 20½ x 42″
Light blue	1 piece 4½ x 42″
Dark blue	2 pieces 1½ x 42″
Light purple	1 piece 2½ x 42″
	*14 squares 2⅜″
Yellow	*14 squares 2⅜″
Applique	8 leaf D, 4 leaf F, 4 bellflowers, 4 small star flowers, 2 side-view columbines, patterns on pages 44-46, see Step 3 for vine
Binding	1 strip 2½″

Directions Use ¼″ seam allowance unless otherwise noted.

1. TRIANGLE BORDER: Make 28 yellow and light purple half square triangle units. Press. Stitch into pairs as shown. Press. Stitch pairs together into a row. Press.

2. ASSEMBLE: Stitch all border pieces together as shown. Press. Stitch border unit to main piece. Press.

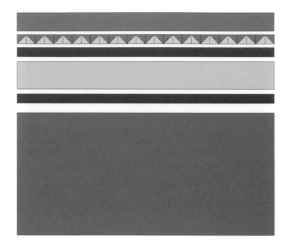

3. APPLIQUE: For vine, bond fusible web to wrong side of 1½ x 18″ piece of dark green. Cut 2 pieces ¼ x 16″. Arrange applique pieces using diagrams as guides, overlapping dark blue borders as desired. Fuse. Stitch in place.

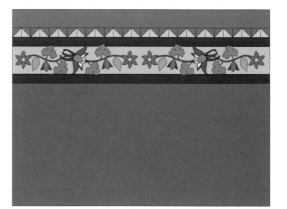

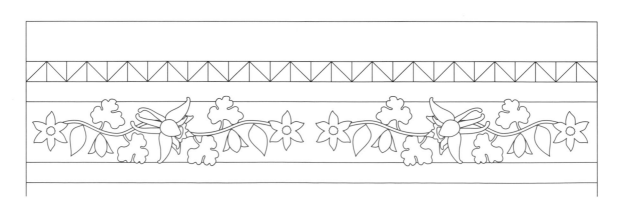

Wildflower Sampler   p 2

4. LAYER & QUILT: Cut backing to same size
    as batting. Layer and quilt as desired. Trim
    backing and batting even with top.

5. FINISH: Fold sham in half, right sides together,
    to 21x29″. Stitch long side and short side
    farthest from applique using ½″ seam
    allowance. Turn right side out. Bind open edge
    using ⅜″ seam allowance.

30 x 41″

Yardage Choose fabrics with 42″ usable width.

Center, Border 3	1 yd black
Flat piping, Border 2	⅜ yd orange
Border 1	⅜ yd blue
	⅙ yd light green
	⅓ yd dark green
Applique	¼ yd each of 1 medium blue (columbines), 1 orange (vase & flower centers)
	⅙ yd each of 3 greens, 1 dark & 1 light blue (columbines), 1 white, 2 oranges (asters)
	⅛ yd each of 2 blues (bellflowers), 1 yellow (flower centers), 1 light & 1 medium purple (bow), 1 pink (star flowers)
Binding	⅜ yd
Backing	1½ yd
Batting	34 x 45″

Cutting Cut strips selvage to selvage.

*Cut in half diagonally. **Cut in quarters diagonally.

Black	1 piece 20 x 30½″ - center
	4 strips 2½″ - Border 3
Orange	3 strips 1″ wide - flat piping
	4 strips 1¼″ - Border 2
Blue	**10 squares 4¾″ - Border 1 side triangles
	*1 square 4⅜″ - Border 1 corner triangles
Light green	20 pieces 1¾ x 3″
Dark green	2 strips 3¼″ wide
	2 pieces 1¾ x 8″ - corners
Applique	1 columbine
	2 side-view columbines
	2 asters
	3 meadow roses
	3 small star flowers
	6 bellflowers
	3 leaf B
	1 & 1 reversed leaf C
	5 leaf E

	1 bow
	stems - see page 47
Binding	4 strips 2½″

Directions
Use ¼″ seam allowance unless otherwise noted.

1. FLAT PIPING: Press strips in half lengthwise, wrong sides together. Cut 2 pieces 30½″ and 2 pieces 20″. With raw edges even, baste long pieces to sides of center panel. Repeat with short pieces at top and bottom.

2. BORDER 1: Follow diagrams for assembly of borders. Stitch borders to quilt, stopping seam lines ¼″ from top left and bottom right corners. Stitch diagonal seams at top left and bottom right. To remaining corners, stitch 8″ dark green strip, centered. Trim each end even with raw edge of border. Stitch blue triangle to each corner. Press. Another diagram on page 38.

TRIANGLE UNITS

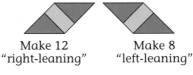

Make 12
"right-leaning"   Make 8
"left-leaning"

STRIP 1 - 3¼″ wide
Make 1st cut at 45° angle from corner.
Cut 10 pieces 1¾″ wide.

STRIP 2 - 3¼″ wide
Make cuts in opposite direction from those in Strip 1. Cut 6.

Sides - "right-leaning"
6 triangle units + 5 trapezoids - Make 2

Top & Bottom - "left-leaning"
4 triangle units + 3 trapezoids - Make 2

Continued on page 38

58x70"

Yardage
Choose fabrics with 42" usable width. Purchase extra yardage if seaming borders diagonally.

Center panel	1⅜ yd large floral
Border 1	¼ yd
Scalloped insert	¾ yd
Border 2	⅞ yd
Border 3	⅓ yd
Applique	⅜ yd light pink, ⅛ yd dark pink, ¼ yd yellow, ⅛ yd dark yellow, ⅙ yd light purple, ⅛ yd dark purple, ⅜ yd green
Border 4	1½ yd
Binding	⅝ yd
Backing	3⅞ yd
Batting	64x76"

Cutting
Cut strips selvage to selvage.

Center panel	1 piece 30½x42½"
Border 1	4 strips 1½" wide
Scalloped insert	52 circles 3¾"
Border 2	5 strips 5½" wide
Border 3	5 strips 1½" wide
Applique	patterns on pages 44-46
	12 asters - pinks
	24 meadow roses - yellows
	8 large star flowers - purples
	see Step 4 for vine
	20 leaf F, 20 leaf F reversed - green
Border 4	6 strips 7½" wide
Binding	7 strips 2½" wide

Directions
Use ¼" seam allowance unless otherwise noted.

1. BORDER 1: Stitch strips end to end. Press. Cut 2 side borders to fit quilt. Stitch to quilt. Press. Repeat at top and bottom.

2. SCALLOPED INSERT: Place 2 circles right sides together. Stitch around entire outside edge. Cut in half, clip, turn, and press.

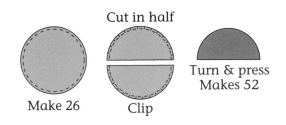

Make 26   Cut in half   Turn & press
                  Clip   Makes 52

Pin and then baste scallops to Border 1, raw edges even, overlapping as needed. Top and bottom have 11 scallops, sides have 15.

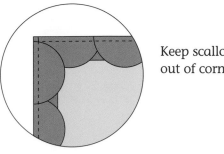

Keep scallops out of corner ¼"

3. BORDERS 2 & 3: Repeat Step 1.

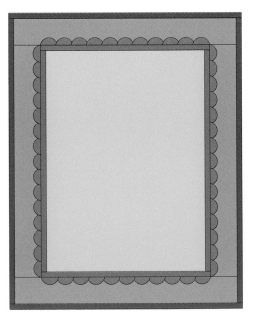

Continued on page 38

45x45"

Yardage
Choose fabrics with 42" usable width.

Cream	¾ yd	3rd star background, tulip border
Light tan	⅜ yd	1st, 2nd, & 4th stars
Medium tan	⅛ yd	1st star points
Medium red	½ yd	1st star bkg, 3rd star points, tulip border
Dark red	⅓ yd	3rd star points, tulip border
Light blue	⅜ yd	4th star background
Medium blue	⅛ yd	2nd star points
Dark blue	1⅛ yd	inner borders, tulip border
Green	½ yd	4th star points, tulip border
Binding	½ yd	
Backing	3 yd	
Batting	49x49"	

Cutting
Cut strips selvage to selvage.
*Cut in half diagonally. **Cut in quarters diagonally.

Cream	4 squares 4½"	3rd star background
	*8 squares 4⅞"	3rd star background
	36 squares 2½"	tulip border background
	*24 squares 2⅞"	tulip border background
Light tan	5 squares 4½"	1st star, 4th star
	4 squares 2½"	2nd star background
	*8 squares 2⅞"	2nd star background
Medium tan	*4 squares 2⅞"	1st star points
Medium red	4 squares 2½"	1st star background
	*16 squares 2⅞"	1st star bkg, tulip border
	*4 squares 4⅞"	3rd star points
Dark red	*4 squares 4⅞"	3rd star points
	12 squares 2½"	tulip border
Light blue	*12 squares 4⅞"	4th star background
Medium blue	*8 squares 2⅞"	2nd star points
Dark blue	2 strips 2½" wide	wide inner border
	4 strips 1½" wide	narrow inner border
	**4 squares 12⅝"	tulip border
Green	*12 squares 4⅞"	4th star points
	*12 squares 2⅞"	tulip border
Binding	5 strips 2¼" wide	

Directions
Use ¼" seam allowance unless otherwise noted.

1. FIRST STAR: Make 1 star block. Press.

Make 8

Make 4

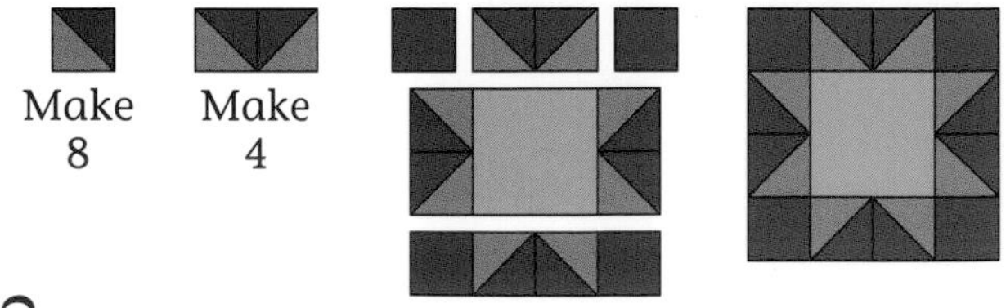

2. SECOND STAR & WIDE INNER BORDER: Make and add units for second star. Cut wide inner border strips into 2 pieces 12½" long and 2 pieces 16½" long. Stitch short pieces to sides of star. Press. Stitch long pieces to top and bottom. Press.

 Make 16

Make 4

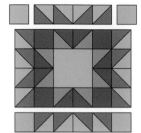

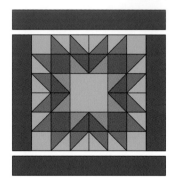

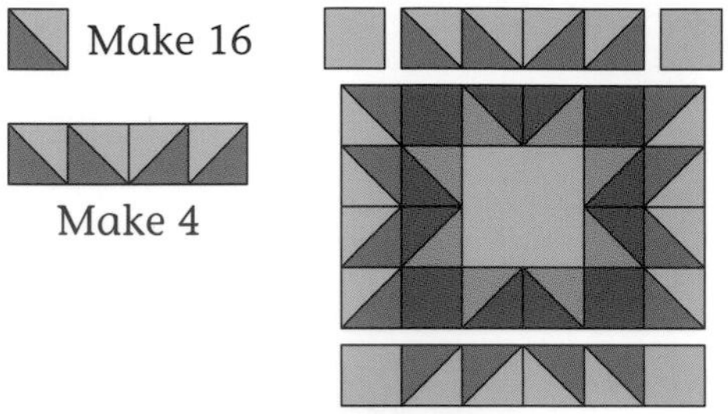

3. THIRD STAR: Make and add units for third star. Press.

Make 8   Make 8   Make 4

4. FOURTH STAR & NARROW INNER BORDER: Make and add units for fourth star. Diagram on page 36. Press. Cut narrow inner border strips into 2 pieces 32½" long and 2 pieces 34½" long. Stitch short pieces to sides of quilt. Press. Stitch long pieces to top and bottom. Press.

Continued on page 36

Long Pillow p 36

55 x 55″   12″ blocks

Note: Quilt in photo has mitered borders to make the bandanna print look better in the corners. Directions are for stairstep borders which works for most fabrics. If you choose to miter the borders, purchase ⅞ yd for Border 1 and cut 6 strips.

Yardage
Choose fabrics with 42″ usable width. Purchase extra yardage if seaming borders diagonally.

Block fabrics, sashing squares

Lt, med, dk red	¼ yd each of 8 or more fabrics
Cream	¼ yd each of 4 or more fabrics
Sashing rectangles	⅔ yd
Border 1	⅔ yd
Border 2	⅝ yd
Binding	⅝ yd
Backing	3⅝ yd
Batting	61x61″

Cutting
Cut strips selvage to selvage.

Blocks	see pages 5-11 - choose 9 blocks
Sashing	24 pieces 2½ x 12½″
	16 squares 2½″
Border 1	5 strips 4″
Border 2	6 strips 2½″
Binding	6 strips 2½″

Directions
Use ¼″ seam allowance unless otherwise noted.

1. BLOCKS: Make 9 blocks using cutting charts and diagrams on pages 5-11. Use photo on page 21 and diagrams on this page for choosing fabrics for each block.

2. SASHING: Stitch 4 sashing squares and 3 sashing rectangles together. Make 4. Press. Stitch 4 sashing rectangles and 3 blocks together. Make 3. Press. Stitch together, alternating sashing and block rows. Press.

3. BORDER 1: Stitch strips end to end. Press. Cut 2 side borders to fit quilt. Stitch to quilt. Press. Repeat at top and bottom.

4. BORDER 2: Repeat Step 3.

5. LAYER & QUILT: Piece backing to same size as batting. Layer and quilt as desired. Trim backing and batting even with top.

6. BIND: Stitch binding strips end to end. Press in half lengthwise, wrong sides together. Bind quilt using ⅜″ seam allowance.

21

56 x 68″   12″ block

Yardage Choose fabrics with 42″ usable width.

Blocks
background	1¾ yd
centers, corners remaining	⅞ yd multicolored floral
patches	¼ yd each of 20 coordinating fabrics
Border 1	⅝ yd
Border 2	⅛ yd each of 8 coordinating fabrics
	¾ yd - outside triangles
Borders 1 & 2	⅛ yd - corner squares
Binding	⅝ yd
Backing	3¾ yd
Batting	62 x 74″

Cutting Cut strips selvage to selvage.
*Cut in half diagonally.

Blocks
background	*120 squares 2⅞″ - corner unit
	80 pieces 2½ x 4½″ - side unit
centers	20 squares 4½″
corners	*40 squares 2⅞″
remaining patches	cut from each fabric:
	4 squares 2½″ - corner unit
	*4 squares 2⅞″ - corner unit
	4 pieces 2½ x 4½″ - side unit
	8 squares 2½″ - side unit
Border 1	6 strips 2½″ wide
Border 2	58 pieces 2½ x 4½″ - coordinating fabrics
	116 squares 2½″ - outside triangles
Borders 1 & 2	8 squares 2½″ - corners
Binding	7 strips 2¼″ wide

Directions Use ¼″ seam allowance unless otherwise noted.

1. BLOCKS: Make 20 blocks using patches randomly. Background, center square and corner triangles are the same in all blocks. Press.

For each block:

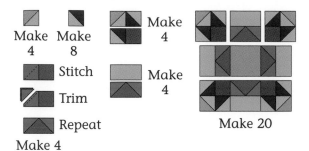

2. ASSEMBLE: Arrange blocks in 5 rows of 4. Stitch into horizontal rows. Press. Stitch rows together. Press.

3. BORDER 1: Stitch strips end to end. Press. Cut 2 side borders to same length as quilt and 2 top/bottom borders to same width as quilt. Stitch side borders to quilt. Press. Stitch squares to each end of top and bottom borders. Press. Stitch top and bottom borders to quilt. Press.

Continued on page 39

76 x 100″   12″ block

Yardage
Choose fabrics with 42″ usable width. Purchase extra yardage if seaming borders diagonally.

Block fabrics for both blocks

Dk blue-purple	1⅛ yd	Block A corner units, Block B center unit
Dk red-purple	2¼ yd	Block B side units
Light blue #1	1⅜ yd	Block A - side units
Light blue #2	1⅜ yd	Block B - side units
Light purple	1 yd	Block B corner & center units
Med purple #1	⅞ yd	Block A corner units
Med purple #2	¾ yd	Block B corner units

Additional Block A fabrics

Choose 8 fabrics graded from light yellow to dark orange. Arrange from lightest to darkest and assign numbers with lightest being #1.

Fabric 1	¼ yd
Fabric 2	½ yd
Fabric 3	⅝ yd
Fabric 4	⅞ yd
Fabric 5	⅔ yd
Fabric 6	½ yd
Fabric 7	⅙ yd
Fabric 8	⅙ yd

Border 1	⅔ yd
Border 2	½ yd
Border 3	1⅝ yd
Binding	⅞ yd
Backing	6¼ yd
Batting	82x106″

Cutting
Cut strips selvage to selvage. *Cut in half diagonally.

Block fabrics for both blocks

Dk blue-purple		
Block A corner units	*36 squares 4⅞″	
Block B center units	34 squares 2½″	
Dk red-purple		
Block B side units	paper piecing	
Light blues		
Both blocks - side units	paper piecing	
Light purple		
Block B corner units	136 squares 2½″	
Block B center units	34 squares 2½″	

Medium purple #1		
Block A corner units	*36 squares 4⅞″	
Medium purple # 2		
Block B corner units	136 squares 2½″	

Additional Block A fabrics for each block - See Step 1

Center Unit	dark	1 square 4½″
	medium	4 squares 2½″
Side Units	light	paper piecing
Border 1	8 strips 2½″	
Border 2	8 strips 1½″	
Border 3	9 strips 5½″	
Binding	9-10 strips 2½″	

Directions
Use ¼″ seam allowance unless otherwise noted.

1. BLOCKS A & B: Following diagrams, make a total of 35 blocks, 18 A and 17 B.

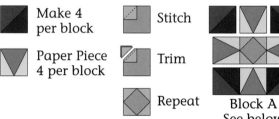

Make 4 per block   Stitch

Paper Piece 4 per block   Trim

Repeat
Make 1 per block

Block A
See below for using additional Block A fabrics

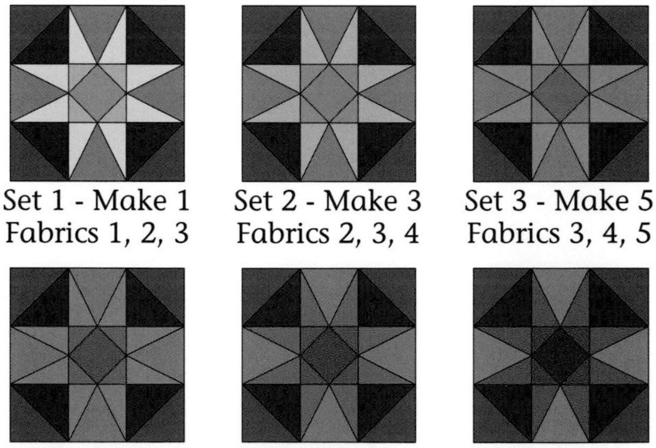

Set 1 - Make 1
Fabrics 1, 2, 3

Set 2 - Make 3
Fabrics 2, 3, 4

Set 3 - Make 5
Fabrics 3, 4, 5

Set 4 - Make 5
Fabrics 4, 5, 6

Set 5 - Make 3
Fabrics 5, 6, 7

Set 6 - Make 1
Fabrics 6, 7, 8

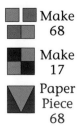

Make 68

Make 17

Paper Piece 68

Block B
Make 17

Continued on page 39

Set of 3, 20 x 20" each   16" Block

Yardage Choose fabrics with 42" usable width.

Background   fat eighths, or ⅙-yd cuts:
    2 each of light yellow, medium
    yellow, dark yellow, light orange,
    medium orange, dark orange, very
    light blue, light blue, medium blue
    note: batiks & graded fabrics yield
    more shades in 1 piece of fabric, &
    it works to use the backs of some
    fabrics for another shade

Border   1⅝ yd white

Applique   ⅓ yd each of 5 or more blues
    ⅙ yd each of 2 yellows
    ⅜ yd white
    ⅓ yd each of 2 greens

Batting   3 pieces 26 x 26" dense flat cotton

Frames   3 frames 20" - black aluminum

Foamcore   3 pieces 20 x 20" - white

Tape   1"-wide white paper art tape

Cutting Cut strips selvage to selvage.

Background   Cut as you sew to control fabric
    placement. Each unit needs:
    2 triangles (cut two 4⅞" squares
    from different fabrics, then cut
    them in half diagonally - use 2
    remaining triangles in other
    units)
    2 squares (cut two 2½" squares
    from different fabrics)

Border   6 pieces 5¼ x 16½"
    6 pieces 5¼ x 26"

Applique   copy patterns on pages 41 & 42
    at 200% - trace 1 set of side view
    flower, 1 set of side view flower
    reversed, 1 set of front view
    flower, 3 large leaves, 3 small
    leaves, 3 small leaves reversed

Directions Use ¼" seam allowance unless otherwise noted.

1. BLOCKS: Arrange fabrics from lightest to
darkest in sets of yellow, orange, and blue.
Pull fabrics from these sets as you cut and sew
1 unit, or 1 diagonal row of units, at a time.
Yellow/orange background squares are graded
on the diagonal from lightest yellows at one
corner to darkest yellows and oranges at
opposite corner. Yellow/orange/blue background square is graded from lightest blue at
one corner to medium blues and oranges at
center to darkest oranges at opposite corner.
Make 2 yellow and orange block backgrounds.
Make 1 yellow, orange, and blue block background. Press.

Units - Make 16 for each background

   Stitch   Trim   Press   Repeat

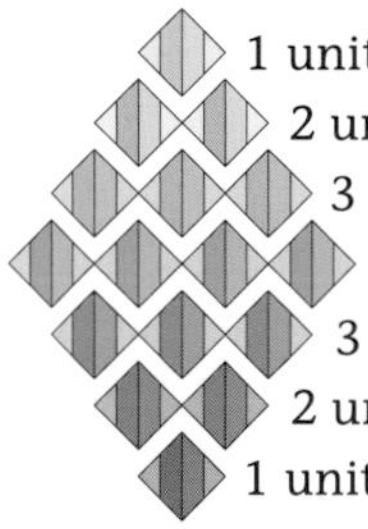

1 unit lightest yellows
2 units light yellows
3 units med & dark yellows
4 units dk yellows & lt oranges
3 units med yellows & oranges
2 units med dk oranges & dk yellow
1 unit darkest oranges & dark yellow

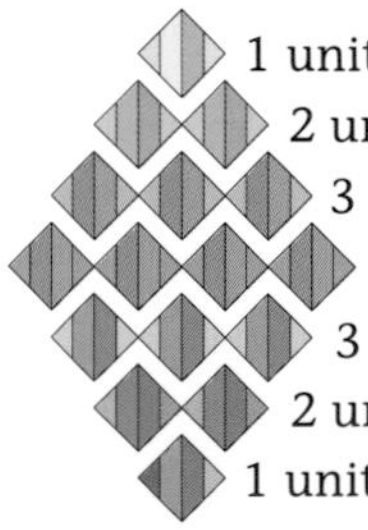

1 unit lightest blues & yellow
2 units light blues
3 units light & med blues
4 units med blues & oranges
3 units med oranges & yellows
2 units med oranges & blue
1 unit darkest oranges

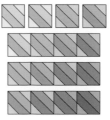

Make 2

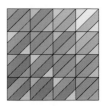

Make 1

Continued on page 37

Mountain Sunrise

Where wild rose and asters twine

and aspen trees do quake,

You'll find the gentle columbine,

Her petals all praise doth take.

skj

The graceful and uniquely petalled Columbine has been the state flower of Colorado since 1899. It seems the perfect representative of our endless blue skies, white mountain peaks and the rich history we have from the gold rush days of Colorado's pioneering and claim-staking history.

The name Aquilegia, the Latin name for Columbine, means eagle. The flowers' long spurs are reminiscent of eagles' talons.

We are all drawn to the beauty of flowers, both wild and abundant on a hillside, or carefully tended in our own small plots of earth. This book is dedicated to the incredible beauty of nature in all her infinite variety and color...and who can appreciate these qualities better than the quilter!

Enjoy!
Lynda Milligan & Nancy Smith

16x44″

Yardage Choose fabrics with 42″ usable width.

Blocks	¼ yd each of 6 or more fabrics
Border/sashing	⅜ yd
Tabs	¼ yd
Binding	⅜ yd
Backing	1½ yd
Batting	20x48″
Buttons	four 1¼″ - optional

Cutting Cut strips selvage to selvage.

Blocks	see pages 5-11 - choose 1-3 blocks
Border/sashing	4 strips 2½″ wide
Tabs	1 strip 4½″ wide
Binding	4 strips 2½″ wide

Directions Use ¼″ seam allowance unless otherwise noted.

1. BLOCKS: Make 3 blocks using cutting charts and diagrams on pages 5-11. Use fabrics as desired.

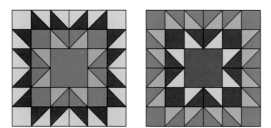

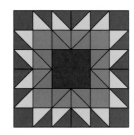

2. BORDER/SASHING: Stitch border/sashing strips end to end. Press. Cut 4 pieces 12½″ long and 2 pieces 44½″ long. Stitch blocks together with short sashing pieces between them. Press. Stitch long pieces to sides. Press.

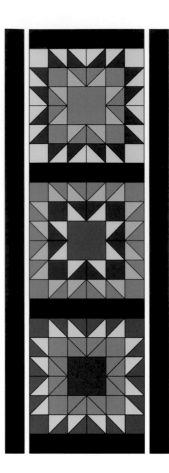

3. LAYER & QUILT: Cut backing to same size as batting. Layer and quilt as desired. Trim backing and batting even with top.

4. TABS: Fold strip in half lengthwise, wrong sides together. Stitch long side. Turn right side out and press with seam in center (rather than at one side). Cut 4 pieces 7″ long. Fold each in half with seam on inside. Pin to back side of top edge of quilt, raw edges together, spaced evenly.

5. BIND: Stitch binding strips end to end. Press in half lengthwise, wrong sides together. Bind quilt using ⅜″ seam allowance, catching tabs in seam. Flip tabs up and tack at each side.

6. OPTIONAL BUTTONS: Stitch buttons to corners with heavy thread.

Long Pillow   p 36

70x90″   12″ blocks

Yardage Choose fabrics with 42″ usable width.

Dark purple	1⅞ yd - blocks, Border 3
Medium purple	¾ yd - Block B, Border 3
Purple/brown print	1⅓ yd - blocks
Gold #1	½ yd - Block A
Gold #2	⅜ yd - Block B
Brown	¾ yd - Block A
Medium blue	1 yd - blocks
Light blue	⅞ yd - Block B, Border 3
Very light blue	1⅜ yd - Block B, Border 3
Border 1	½ yd
Border 2	1¼ yd
Binding	¾ yd
Backing	5¾ yd
Batting	76x96″

Cutting Cut strips selvage to selvage.
*Cut in half diagonally. **Cut in quarters diagonally.

Dark purple	*30 squares 4⅞″ - Block A
	**30 squares 5¼″ - Block B
	**15 squares 5¼″ - Border 3
	4 pieces 1½x4½″ - Border 3
Medium purple	**15 squares 5¼″ - Block B
	**8 squares 5¼″ - Border 3
Purple/brown print	15 squares 4½″ - Block A
	60 pieces 2½x4½″ - Block A
	60 squares 2½″ - Block B
Gold #1	*30 squares 3¾″ - Block A
Gold #2	15 squares 4½″ - Block B
Brown	*90 squares 2⅞″ - Block A
Medium blue	*90 squares 2⅞″ - Block A
	60 squares 2½″ - Block B
Light blue	*30 squares 4⅞″ - Block B
	4 squares 4½″ - Border 3
Very light blue	*30 squares 4⅞″ - Block B
	**15 squares 5¼″ - Block B
	**8 squares 5¼″ - Border 3
Border 1	7 strips 1½″ wide
Border 2	8 strips 4½″ wide
Binding	9 strips 2¼″ wide

Directions Use ¼″ seam allowance unless otherwise noted.

1. BLOCKS: Make 15 Block A and 15 Block B following diagrams. Press.

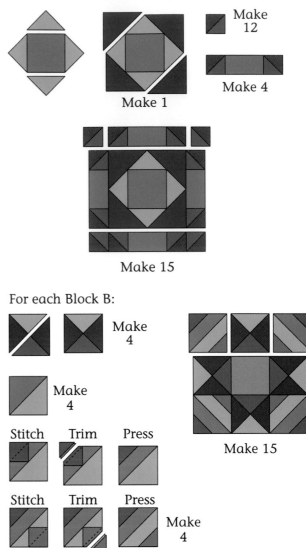

For each Block A:

Make 12

Make 4

Make 1

Make 15

For each Block B:

Make 4

Make 4

Stitch   Trim   Press

Stitch   Trim   Press   Make 4

Make 15

2. ASSEMBLE: Placing blocks in alternating positions, stitch into horizontal rows. Press. Stitch rows together. Press. Diagram on page 37.

Continued on page 37

Set of 3, 18x18″ each

Yardage Choose fabrics with 42″ usable width.

Center square	½ yd each of 3 fabrics
Border 1	⅛ yd each of 3 fabrics
Border 2	¼ yd each of 3 fabrics
Applique	½ yd light brown - branches
	¼ yd blue - large part of columbine
	⅙ yd blue - meadow roses
	⅙ yd pink - large part of aster
	⅙ yd white - columbine center
	⅛ yd each - 2-3 greens, 1 yellow, 1 orange (aster center), desired colors for circles
Binding	⅝ yd
Backing	1⅜ yd
Batting	3 pieces 20x20″

Cutting Cut strips selvage to selvage.

Center square	1 square 12½″ of each fabric
Border 1	2 strips 1″ wide of each fabric
Border 2	2 strips 3″ wide of each fabric
Applique	patterns on pages 40, 44-45 3 sets of branches, 1 columbine, 1 aster, 4 meadow roses, 1 meadow rose at 200%, leaves & circles as desired
Binding	6 strips 2½″ wide

Directions Use ¼″ seam allowance unless otherwise noted.

1. CENTER SQUARE: Fuse branches to center squares. Applique in place.

2. BORDERS: For each hanging, cut 2 pieces 12½″ long and 2 pieces 13½″ long from Border 1 strips. Stitch short pieces to sides of center squares. Press. Repeat at top and bottom with long pieces. From Border 2 strips, cut 2 pieces 13½″ long and 2 pieces 18½″ long from Border 2 strips. Stitch to hangings.

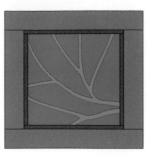

3. APPLIQUE: Fuse flowers, leaves, and circles to hangings. Applique in place.

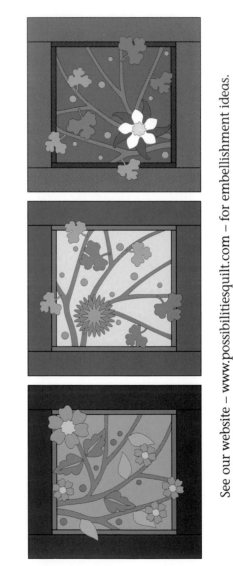

4. LAYER & QUILT: Cut 3 backing pieces 20x20″. Layer and quilt as desired. Trim backing and batting even with top.

5. BIND: Stitch 2 binding strips end to end for each hanging. Press in half lengthwise, wrong sides together. Bind using ⅜″ seam allowance.

See our website – www.possibilitiesquilt.com – for embellishment ideas.

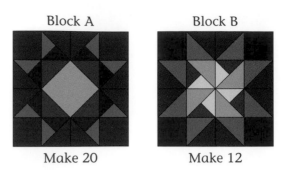

Block A   Block B

Make 20   Make 12

73x90″

Yardage Choose fabrics with 42″ usable width.

Blocks	½ yd each of 4 blacks
	⅔ yd each of 4 dark browns
	⅓ yd each of 4 rusts
	½ yd each of 4 dark golds
	⅜ yd each of 4 light golds
	⅜ yd cream - center pinwheel Block B
Setting triangles	1½ yd black
Border 1	⅜ yd brown stripe
Border 2	¾ yd brown
Binding	¾ yd
Backing	5¾ yd
Batting	79x96″

Cutting Cut strips selvage to selvage.
*Cut in half diagonally. **Cut in quarters diagonally.

Blocks

Block A side units	**10 squares 4¼″ from each BLACK
Block B corners	12 squares 3½″ from each BLACK
Blocks A & B side units	*32 squares 3⅞″ from each BROWN
Block A corners	20 squares 3½″ from each BROWN
Block A center unit	*10 squares 3⅞″ from each RUST
Block B center unit	**3 squares 4¼″ from each RUST
Block A side units	**10 squares 4¼″ from each DARK GOLD
Block B side units	*12 squares 3⅞″ from each DARK GOLD
Block A center unit	5 squares 4¾″ from each LIGHT GOLD
Block B center unit	*6 squares 3⅞″ from each LIGHT GOLD
Block B center unit	**12 squares 4¼″ CREAM
Setting triangles	*2 squares 9⅜″ - corners
	**4 squares 18¼″ - sides
Border 1	8 strips 1⅛″ wide
Border 2	8-9 strips 2½″ wide
Binding	9 strips 2½″ wide

Directions Use ¼″ seam allowance unless otherwise noted.

1. BLOCKS: Use as many different fabrics in each block as possible with the exception of small cream triangles in center of Block B, which are all one fabric. For Block A, use diagrams for Block 12 on page 10. Make 20. Press. For Block B, use diagrams for Block 11 on page 10. Make 12. Press.

2. ASSEMBLE: Arrange blocks on point, alternating Block A and Block B. Arrange setting triangles around blocks. Stitch blocks and setting triangles in diagonal rows. Press. Stitch rows together. Press.

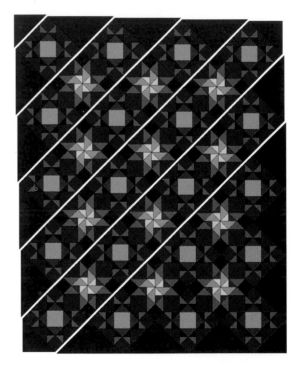

3. BORDERS 1 & 2: Stitch Border 1 strips end to end. Press. Cut 2 pieces to fit sides of quilt. Stitch to sides of quilt. Press. Repeat at top and bottom. Repeat with Border 2 strips.

4. LAYER & QUILT: Piece backing vertically to same size as batting. Layer and quilt as desired. Trim backing and batting even with top.

5. BIND: Stitch binding strips end to end. Press in half lengthwise, wrong sides together. Bind quilt using ⅜″ seam allowance.

Long Pillow

28x14″ Photos on pages 19 & 29

Supplies Choose fabrics with 42″ usable width.

Block centers, center panel	¼ yd
Inner star points, center panel	⅛ yd
Inner star background	¼ yd
Outer star points, center panel	¼ yd
Outer star background	¼ yd
Center panel	⅛ yd
Backing for quilting	⅝ yd
Border, envelope back	1 yd
Batting	32x18″
Velcro® strip	⅙ yd
Pillow form	14x28″

Cutting Cut strips selvage to selvage.
*Cut in half diagonally.

Block centers, center panel	2 squares 4½″
	* 2 squares 2⅞″
Inner star points, center panel	*12 squares 2⅞″
Inner star background	8 squares 2½″
	*8 squares 2⅞″
Outer star points, center panel	*22 squares 2⅞″
Outer star background	8 squares 2½″
	*14 squares 2⅞″
Center panel	2 squares 2⅞″
Border, envelope back	2 pieces 1½x28½″
	2 pieces 20x28½″

Directions Use ¼″ seam allowance unless otherwise noted.

1. PILLOW TOP: Make 2 blocks and 1 center panel following diagrams. Press. Stitch blocks and center panel together. Press. Stitch border pieces to top and bottom. Press.

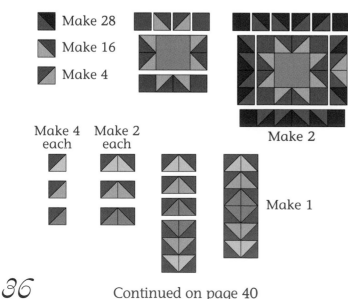

Make 28
Make 16
Make 4

Make 4 each
Make 2 each
Make 2
Make 1

Plantation Star
Continued from page 18

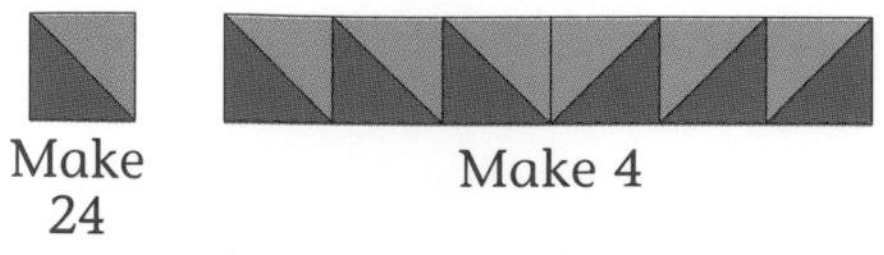

Make 24
Make 4

5. TULIP BORDER: Make 12 triangle units. Press. Stitch into 4 borders with blue triangles. Press. Stitch to quilt. Press. Make 4 corners. Press. Stitch to quilt. Press.

Make 24
Make 12
Make 4
Make 4

6. LAYER & QUILT: Piece backing to same size as batting. Layer and quilt as desired. Trim backing and batting even with top.

7. BIND: Stitch binding strips end to end. Press in half lengthwise, wrong sides together. Bind quilt using ¼″ seam allowance.

 Continued on page 40

Indiglow
Continued from page 30

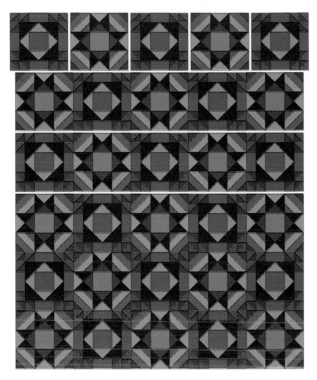

3. BORDER 1: Stitch strips end to end. Press. Cut 2 side borders to same length as quilt. Stitch to sides of quilt. Press. Repeat at top and bottom.

4. BORDER 2: Repeat Step 3.

5. BORDER 3: Make 30 units. Diagram on page 41. Press. Stitch 15 units, corner squares, and spacer rectangles into border as shown. Press. Make 2. Stitch one to top and one to bottom of quilt with medium purple triangles to outside of quilt. Press.

6. LAYER & QUILT: Piece backing vertically to same size as batting. Layer and quilt as desired. Trim backing and batting even with top.

7. BIND: Stitch binding strips end to end. Press in half lengthwise, wrong sides together. Bind quilt using ¼″ seam allowance.

Mountain Sunrise
Continued from page 26

2. BORDER: Orient color in blocks as shown below. Stitch short border pieces to sides of background squares. Press. Repeat at top and bottom with long pieces.

3. APPLIQUE: Machine applique flowers using photo and diagrams as guides.

4. LAYER & QUILT: Layer top and batting—no backing needed. Quilt as desired no more than 2″ into border so batting can be trimmed afterwards. Enhance leaves and flowers with thread painting, if desired. Fold back top and trim batting to 20″ square. This should be approximately 2″ from seam between border and background on each side. Test and mark before cutting.

5. Stretch over foamcore and tape in place on back. Insert in frame following manufacturer's directions.

Secret Garden
Continued from page 16

4. BORDER 4:

Stitch border strips end to end. Press. Cut 2 pieces 56½″ long and 2 pieces 58½″ long. Mark center of each.

For vine, apply fusible web to wrong side of 5x12″ piece of green fabric following manufacturer's directions. Cut 16 pieces ¼x12″.

Place vine segments as shown, then largest flowers, then smallest flowers and leaves. Area covered is approximately 6x42″. When all is arranged, fuse. Machine applique edges. See diagrams on page 43.

Stitch short borders to sides, facing as shown. Press. Repeat at top and bottom with long borders.

5. LAYER & QUILT: Piece backing horizontally to same size as batting. Layer and quilt as desired. Trim backing and batting even with top.

6. BIND: Stitch binding strips end to end. Press in half lengthwise, wrong sides together. Bind quilt using ⅜″ seam allowance.

Fresh Picked
Continued from page 14

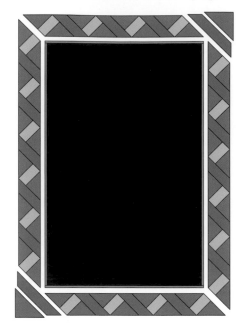

3. BORDERS 2 & 3: Cut 2 side borders to fit quilt. Stitch to quilt. Press. Repeat at top and bottom.

4. APPLIQUE: Applique vase and bouquet to center panel, centered in each direction. Use photo and diagram as guides. See pages 43-46 for patterns and page 47 for layout diagrams and directions. After applique pieces are arranged, but before fusing, trim stems to just below top of vase.

5. LAYER & QUILT: Cut backing to same size as batting. Layer and quilt as desired. Trim backing and batting even with top.

6. BIND: Stitch binding strips end to end. Press in half lengthwise, wrong sides together. Bind quilt using ⅜″ seam allowance.

Rising Stars

Continued from page 24

2. ASSEMBLE: Place blocks in positions shown in diagram—Set 1 of Block A at top left, Block B blocks in next diagonal row, Set 2 of Block A in next diagonal row, and so on. Stitch blocks into horizontal rows. Press. Stitch rows together. Press.

3. BORDERS 1-3: Stitch strips end to end. Press. Cut 2 side borders to fit quilt. Stitch to quilt. Press. Repeat at top and bottom.

4. LAYER & QUILT: Piece backing vertically to same size as batting. Layer and quilt as desired. Trim backing and batting even with top.

5. BIND: Stitch binding strips end to end. Press in half lengthwise, wrong sides together. Bind quilt using 3/8" seam allowance.

Toast & Jam

Continued from page 22

4. BORDER 2: Make 58 units. Press. Stitch units into borders as shown. Stitch side borders to quilt. Press. Stitch corner squares to each end of top and bottom borders. Stitch to quilt. Press.

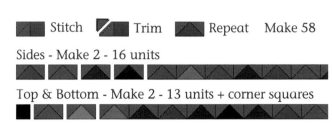

5. LAYER & QUILT: Piece backing horizontally to same size as batting. Layer and quilt as desired. Trim backing and batting even with top.

6. BIND: Stitch binding strips end to end. Press in half lengthwise, wrong sides together. Bind quilt using 1/4" seam allowance.

Branches

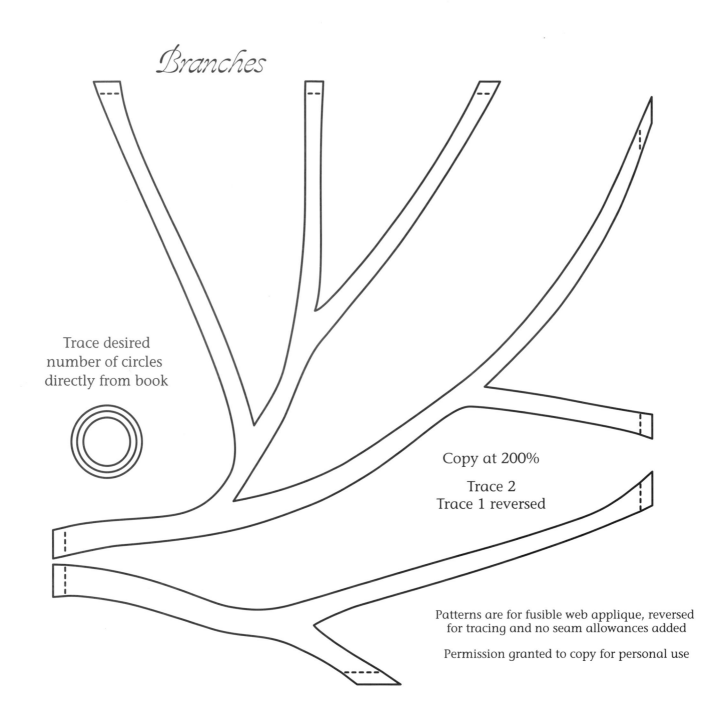

Trace desired
number of circles
directly from book

Copy at 200%

Trace 2
Trace 1 reversed

Patterns are for fusible web applique, reversed
for tracing and no seam allowances added

Permission granted to copy for personal use

Long Pillow

Continued from page 36

2. LAYER & QUILT: Cut backing for quilting to same size as batting. Layer and quilt as desired. Trim backing and batting even with top.

3. ENVELOPE BACK: Press pieces in half lengthwise, wrong sides together (10x28½"). Place both on right side of pillow front, raw edges matching, folded edges overlapping in center. Stitch around entire outside edge. Clip corners, turn right side out. Cut Velcro® in 2 pieces. Place pillow cover on pillow form and work out placement for Velcro®. Mark placement. Remove pillow form. Stitch Velcro® to pillow opening.

Stem
Apply fusible web to
wrong side of 1x16" piece
of green fabric following
manufacturer's directions.
Cut 1 piece ½ x 15".

Mountain Sunrise

Copy at 200%
Trace 1

Light yellow

Dark yellow

Light blue

Dark blue

White

Medium blue

Medium green

Dark green

Patterns are for fusible web applique, reversed
for tracing and no seam allowances added
Permission granted to copy for personal use

Copy at 200%
Trace 3,
trace 3 reversed

Indiglow
Continued from page 37

Make 30

Make 2

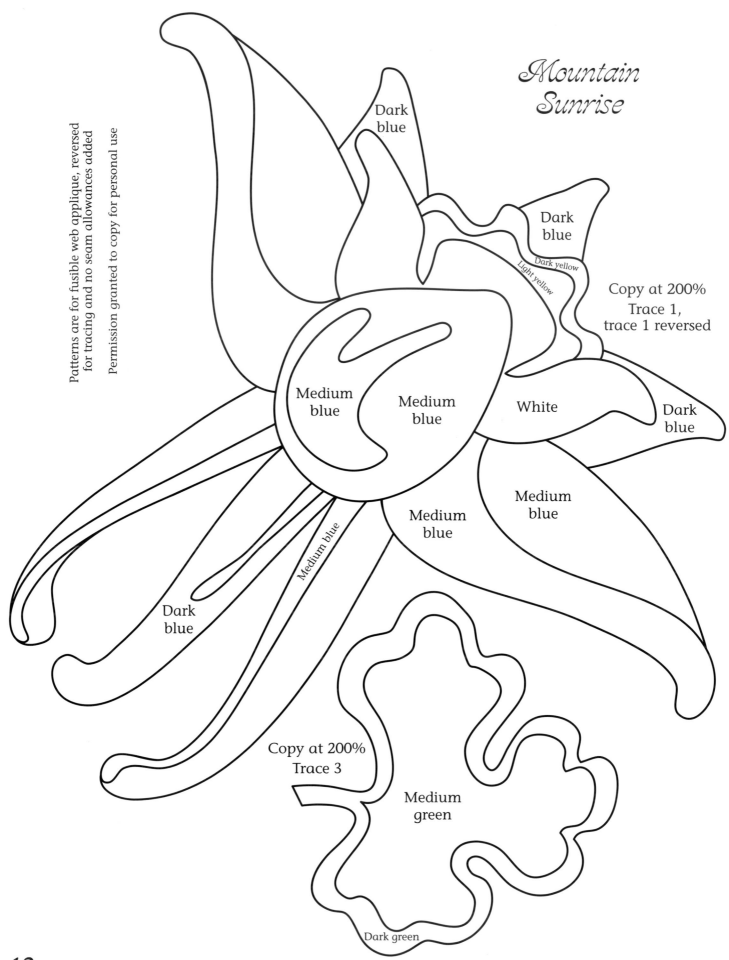

Mountain
Sunrise

Dark
blue

Dark
blue

Dark yellow

Light yellow

Copy at 200%
Trace 1,
trace 1 reversed

Patterns are for fusible web applique, reversed
for tracing and no seam allowances added

Permission granted to copy for personal use

Medium
blue

Medium
blue

White

Dark
blue

Medium
blue

Medium
blue

Medium blue

Dark
blue

Copy at 200%
Trace 3

Medium
green

Dark green

42

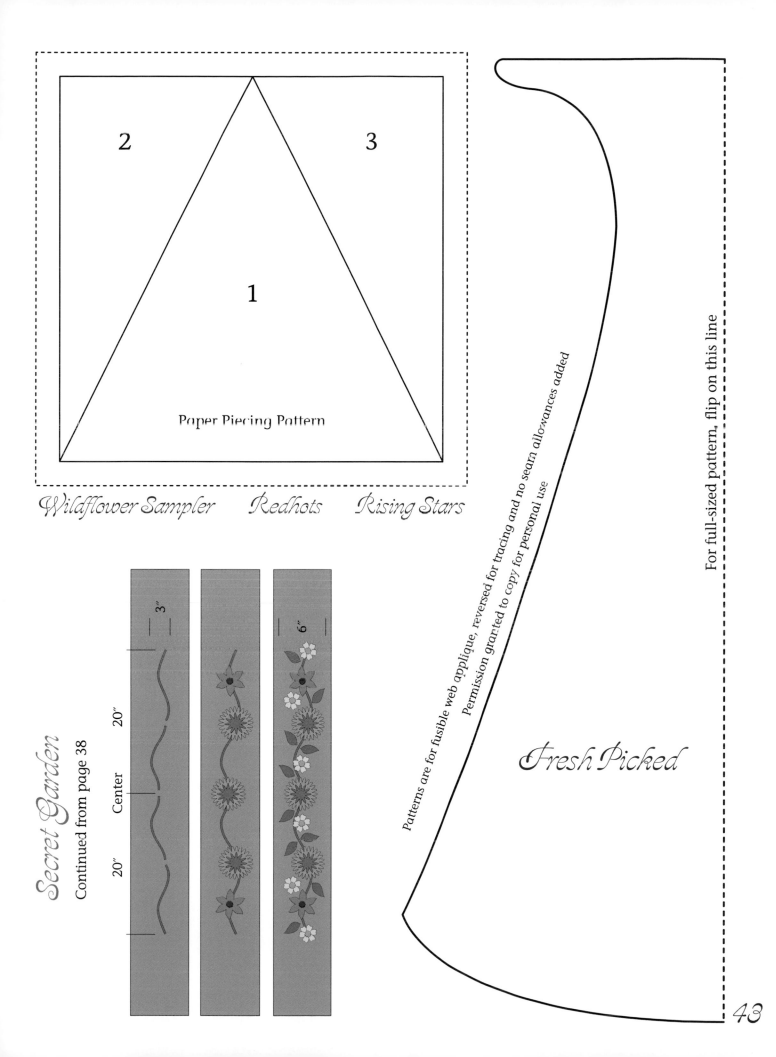

2

3

1

Paper Piecing Pattern

Wildflower Sampler   Redhots   Rising Stars

Secret Garden

Continued from page 38

20"   20"   Center   20"   20"

3"

6"

Patterns are for fusible web applique, reversed for tracing and no seam allowances added

Permission granted to copy for personal use

For full-sized pattern, flip on this line

Fresh Picked

Wildflower
Sampler

Fresh Picked

Columbine

White

Blue

Yellow

Bellflower

Branches
Secret Garden

Darkest blue

Darkest blue

Yellow

White

White

White

Medium
blue

Lightest
blue

Medium
blue

Meadow
Rose

Side-View
Columbine

Darkest
blue

Patterns are for fusible web applique, reversed
for tracing and no seam allowances added

44

Leaves

A
Border

B
Center Panel

Wildflower Sampler

Fresh Picked

Secret Garden

Branches

Berry

D
Border

C
Center Panel

Patterns are for
fusible web applique,
reversed for tracing and
no seam allowances added

Permission granted to
copy for personal use

E
Center Panel

F
Border

Aster

45

Wildflower Sampler
Fresh Picked
Secret Garden

Small Star
Flower

Omit heart
for Fresh Picked

Large
Star
Flower

Trace right side
of bow in reverse

Patterns are for fusible web applique, reversed
for tracing and no seam allowances added

46

Permission granted to copy for personal use

Wildflower Sampler
Fresh Picked

Placement Diagram

Center Panel Layout

See directions at lower left for fusing & cutting stems. Cut stems to lengths shown on diagram below. Place stems first, then add largest flowers. Next, place smaller flowers. Then place leaves, tucking some under other pieces. Last, place bow. When all is arranged, fuse.

Permission granted to copy for personal use

25″
22″   22″
20″   17″   20″
15″
18″   18″

Stems cover an area approximately 15 x 26″, centered from side to side & about 4″ from seam at bottom of center panel (2¼″ for Fresh Picked)

Finished bouquet covers an area approximately 18 x 28″, about 4″ from seams at top & bottom of center panel, about 2″ from seams at sides of center panel (1″ from all seam lines for Fresh Picked)

Stems
Apply fusible web to wrong side of 2 x 27″ pieces of dark, medium, and medium light greens following manufacturer's directions. From each fabric, cut 3 pieces ¼ x 26″.

Wildflower Sampler

Vines

For vines, apply fusible web to wrong side of 4 x 40″ piece of dark green following manufacturer's directions. Cut 6 pieces ¼ x 40″.

Border Layout

Cut vines to lengths shown on diagram below. Place vines first, then add largest flowers. Next, place smaller flowers. Then place leaves, tucking some under other pieces. When all is arranged, fuse.

Placement Diagram

10″

9″

8″

Vines from corner to one end cover an area approximately 3½ x 26″, centered on border

8″ 9″ 10″ 3½″

26″

Finished applique from corner to one end covers an area approximately 7 x 30″, centered on border

7″

30″

48